DO IT YOURSELF

Healthy Eating

Diet and Nutrition

Anna Claybourne

Heinemann Library

Chicago, Illinois

Customer Service 888-454-2279
Visit our website at www.heinemannraintree.com

Editorial: Louise Galpine and Kate deVilliers
Design: Richard Parker and Tinstar Design Ltd
Illustrations: Oxford designers & illustrators
Picture Research: Mica Brancic and Elaine Willis
Production: Victoria Fitzgerald

Originated by Chroma Graphics (Overseas) Pte. Ltd
Printed and bound in China by Leo Paper Group

12 11 10 09 08
10 9 8 7 6 5 4 3 2 1

Library of Congress Cataloging-in-Publication Data
Claybourne, Anna.
Healthy eating : diet and nutrition / Anna Claybourne.
   p. cm. -- (Do it yourself science)
Includes bibliographical references and index.
ISBN 978-1-4329-1085-3 (hc) -- ISBN 978-1-4329-1101-0 (pb) 1. Nutrition--Juvenile literature. I. Title.
RA784.C552 2008
613.2--dc22
                                2007050622

Acknowledgments
The publishers would like to thank the following for permission to reproduce photographs:
©Alamy pp. **4** (Ace Stock Ltd), **13** (Foodfolio); ©Corbis pp. **8** (Albrecht G. Schaefer), **11** (Owen Franken), **16** (photocuisine/Sirois), **24** (Anders Ryman), **27** (Bob Krist), **30** (Picture Arts/Jack Andersen), **33** (Reuters/China Photo), **37** (Tom Stewart), **38** (David Stoecklein), **42** (Brooke Fasani); ©Getty Images pp. **5** (Tony Anderson), **7** (The Image Bank/Terje Rakke), **9** (Alistair Berg), **15** (Rita Maas), **17** (Elie Bernager), **19** (Neo Vision), **21** (Dorling Kindersely), **23** (Rosemary Weller), **25** (Photographer's Choice/Noel Hendrickson), **29** (Britt Erlanson), **35** (StockFood Creative/David Loftus), **40-41** (PhotoDisc), **43** (Stone/Lori Adamski Peek); ©Pearson Education Ltd pp. **40** (Rob Judges, 2005), **40-41** (Tudor Photography); ©Rex Features p. **39** (Image Source).

Cover photograph of a red apple, reproduced with permission of ©Corbis / Danilo Calilung.

Every effort has been made to contact copyright holders of any material reproduced in this book.
Any omissions will be rectified in subsequent printings if notice is given to the publishers.

Contents

Any words appearing in the text in bold, **like this**, are explained in the glossary.

Why Do We Eat?

Eating is a big part of everyone's lives. We have food and drinks several times each day, and most people love eating. At parties and celebrations, we share food with our family and friends.

Food is not just for pleasure, though. Everyone needs to eat to stay alive. Without food, our bodies would stop working. Eating healthily means eating the best foods to help your body.

Here are just a few of the thousands of healthy foods you can eat.

Food and your body

Food gives your body the **chemicals** it needs to work properly. Chemicals are substances that make up food, your body, and other matter. For example, there are chemicals in beans and meat that help your body to grow hair and fingernails. A chemical found in bananas helps you to sleep well at night.

Food also gives your body energy. It acts like fuel in a car, giving you the power to move around and do things. Foods that contain a lot of energy include pasta, raisins, and nuts.

Cook safely

Preparing food is fun, but be careful! You sometimes need to use a sharp knife or a hot stove. Where you see this sign, be extra careful and make sure you have an adult to help you.

Apples make a great healthy snack. They contain water, carbohydrates, fiber, and vitamins.

Digesting food

Everyone has a **digestive system**. This is a set of body parts that take in food, break it down, and collect all the useful chemicals your body needs. The digestive system also collects food waste, which is eliminated from your body when you go to the bathroom.

Food groups

There are thousands of different foods. But they can be divided into just a few main types that do different jobs. These are called **food groups**.

Food group	Characteristics	Group includes
Carbohydrates	Provide energy	Bread, pasta, rice, **sugar**, and sugary foods
Protein	Builds body parts and repairs injuries	Meat, eggs, **dairy products**, beans, lentils
Fat	Provides energy, helps the brain work, keeps skin and hair healthy	Meat, cream, butter, oils, and some fish, nuts, and seeds
Fiber	Helps the digestive system to work	Whole **grains**, nuts, seeds, **fruits**, and **vegetables**
Vitamins and **minerals**	Help the body in many different ways	In many foods including fruits and vegetables, dairy products, and meat

Starting the Day

Steps to follow

Power porridge

To make porridge for two people, you will need:

* 1 cup porridge oats
* 1 cup water
* 1 cup milk
* A handful of raisins (optional)
* Small saucepan
* Wooden spoon

1 Pour the oats into the saucepan, then add the water and milk and stir well.

2 ⚠ Put the saucepan over medium heat and stir until the porridge starts to boil and bubble (about two minutes).

3 Add the raisins if you are using them. Turn down the heat and stir for another two minutes. To serve, pour the porridge into bowls. You could add a little extra milk to cool it down and a little honey or extra raisins to make it sweeter, if you like.

What's in porridge?

Oats are the main ingredient of porridge. They are a type of **grain**, such as wheat, rice, and corn. Grains are also known as **cereals**. They are a type of plant seed. They contain several types of **carbohydrate**—food **chemicals** that are full of energy and give your body fuel. Around the world, most people eat some kind of cereal every day. In Asia rice is very common, in the United States people eat a lot of wheat or corn, and in Africa people often eat cereals called millet and sorghum.

Farm machinery separates the edible grains, such as these oat grains, from the other parts of the plant they grow on.

Slow-release energy

Oats are an amazing food. They release energy into your body very slowly. That is why porridge made from oats is a great food to have for breakfast. It keeps on giving you energy for several hours, so you can keep going until lunchtime.

Raisins

Raisins are dried grapes. Adding raisins to your porridge makes it sweeter and provides extra energy. The raisins also contain **fiber**, **vitamins**, and **minerals**.

Staple foods

Foods such as cereals are sometimes called staple foods. Potatoes are a staple food, too, although they are not grains.

Staple foods are foods that we eat every day, and that form a main part of our **diet**. They contain carbohydrates that give us the energy we need to keep going all day long.

In fact, to be healthy, at least one-third of your food should be staple foods such as bread, potatoes, pasta, or rice. Many meals, such as sandwiches or pasta salad, are based around a staple food.

Millions of people around the world eat bread every day. This woman in India is making chapatis, a type of flat bread.

Whole or refined?

Cereals can be **whole-grain** or **refined**. "Whole-grain" means that all of the grain in its natural state is put into the food. "Refined" means that some parts of the grain, such as the **husk** and **bran** (the outer coverings of the grain), are removed. For example, whole-wheat bread is made with whole-grain wheat, and white bread is made with refined wheat. Whole-grain cereals are healthier because they contain more fiber, vitamins, and minerals.

In your body

Staple foods come from plants. They are the parts of the plant where energy is stored as chemicals. When you eat them, your body takes these complex chemicals and breaks them down into a simpler chemical called **glucose**. Glucose contains energy in a form your body can use. Your blood carries glucose around your body, delivering energy to all your body parts and **cells** (the tiny units that make up your body). Your body uses energy to make its parts move and function.

Healthy breakfasts

Breakfast is a very important meal. It is the first thing you eat after a long night sleeping. Eating a healthy breakfast gives you energy for the day. It also stops you from getting too hungry and overeating later on. Having cereal for breakfast is a good idea because of the energy it contains. Other good breakfast foods include **fruit**, yogurt, and eggs.

The carbohydrates in whole-grain cereals give you long-lasting energy.

Fun fruit pancakes

For four people, you will need:

* 2 cups whole-wheat flour
* 2 teaspoons baking powder
* 2 eggs
* 1 cup low-fat yogurt
* 1 cup 2% milk
* 1 cup fruit (such as blueberries, raspberries, chopped apple, or pineapple)
* A little sunflower oil
* Large bowl
* Flour sifter
* Whisk
* Ladle
* Frying pan
* Spatula
* Paper towels

A healthy mix

These pancakes make a good breakfast. The flour contains carbohydrates, fiber, and vitamins. The egg is full of **protein**. The yogurt and milk contain protein and **calcium**, which is good for teeth and bones. The fruit contains fiber, vitamins, and minerals.

1 Sift the flour and baking powder into a large bowl. Break the eggs into the bowl, then add the yogurt and milk. Whisk together. Gently stir in the fruit.

2 Put the frying pan over medium heat and add about two teaspoons of oil. Take a ladleful of pancake mixture and pour it into the pan to make each pancake. You can fit several pancakes in the pan at once.

3 After about one minute, use the spatula to turn the pancakes over. Cook for another minute. Lift the pancakes out and lay them on a piece of paper towel. Now cook the rest.

Fats and frying

Frying is cooking food in hot **fat**. You should only eat a little fat in your diet, because too much can be harmful for you. When frying foods, you should use just a little fat in the pan.

Olive oil is made by pressing olives to squeeze the oil out.

Healthy and not-so-healthy fat

There are several types of fat. Some are good for you, but some are not. Solid fats from animal products, such as butter, are less healthy. **Trans-fats** or **hydrogenated fats** have been changed to make them easier to cook with. They are unhealthy, too. They can build up in your body and damage your heart.

The healthiest fats are liquid oils, such as olive oil and sunflower oil. Fats found in nuts and in **oil-rich fish**, such as mackerel, are also healthy fats. Healthy fats are good for your heart and brain.

Main Meals

Steps to follow

Chunky kebabs

For four people, you will need:

* 1 pound chicken breast fillets
* 1 red or green pepper
* 1½ cups button mushrooms
* Juice of half a lemon
* A small pinch of salt and a grind of pepper

For the marinade:

* ½ cup olive oil
* 1 tablespoon tomato puree
* 1 tablespoon honey
* 1 teaspoon minced garlic
* Large bowl
* Lemon juicer
* Sharp knife
* Chopping board
* Wooden spoon
* Kebab skewers
* Cooking tongs
* Grill pan

1 Mix the marinade ingredients together in the bowl. Cut the chicken into bite-sized chunks. Add them to the marinade, then wash your hands. Stir the chicken into the marinade and leave in the refrigerator for an hour.

2 Wash the pepper and mushrooms. Cut the pepper into 2-inch (5-cm) squares. Take the chicken pieces out of the marinade and thread one piece on to each skewer, then thread on a mushroom and a pepper slice. Repeat until all the ingredients have been used up. Then wash your hands again.

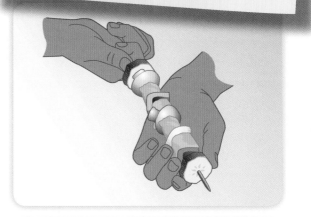

3 To cook the kebabs, place them on a medium-hot grill. Cook for about 12 to 15 minutes, turning frequently. Before eating the kebabs, check that the chicken is done. Cut open the largest chunk of chicken. It should be white all the way through, with no pink.

What is meat?

Meat, such as chicken, is the flesh of an animal. Meat contains lots of **protein**. Your body uses protein to build body parts such as muscle and hair, to repair injuries, and to grow. Meat also contains **minerals** your body needs. **Iron** is a mineral found in meat that helps your blood to carry oxygen.

Healthy grills

Grilling is a very healthy way to cook meat. Some of the **fat** in the meat drains away as it cooks, which means you eat less of it.

Handling meat safely

Raw meat can contain **germs** that can make you sick. Follow these safety tips:

- Keep raw meat away from other foods.
- Wash chopping boards, knives, plates, and anything else that has touched raw meat before using them again.
- Wash your hands well after touching raw meat.
- Always make sure meat is cooked all the way through.

You could have your kebab with bread or baked potatoes. You could even eat it as a wrap, rolled up inside a flour tortilla.

Steps to follow

1 Put 1 cup of boiling water in the bowl and add the cous cous. Stir, cover with a pan lid, and leave for 10 minutes. Then stir it with a fork.

2 Open the tuna and beans and drain off the liquid. Stir the tuna and beans into the prepared cous cous. Wash, prepare, and chop the salad vegetables. Stir them into the cous cous.

Everything salad

For four people, you will need:

* 1 cup cous cous
* 1 cup boiling water
* 1 can tuna chunks in water
* 1 can cooked kidney beans or other beans
* Selection of salad **vegetables**. Choose from the following:
  * Half a cucumber, chopped
  * 1 red or green pepper, deseeded and chopped
  * 4 green onions, peeled and chopped
  * 2 tomatoes, chopped
  * 2 sticks of celery, chopped
  * A handful of fresh parsley, finely chopped

For the dressing:

* 1/4 cup olive oil
* 1 tablespoon balsamic or white wine vinegar
* 1 tablespoon tomato puree
* 1 teaspoon honey
* A small pinch of salt and a grind of pepper

Utensils:

* Measuring cup (for liquids)
* Pan lid
* Large heatproof bowl
* Can opener
* Fork
* Sharp knife
* Chopping board
* Jar with lid

3 Put all the dressing ingredients into the jar and screw the lid on. Shake well and stir the dressing into the salad.

Raw or cooked?

Cooking, especially for a long time, can destroy the healthy **vitamins** in some foods. But sometimes cooking a food makes it healthier. Tomatoes contain a **chemical** called **lycopene**, which helps prevent diseases such as cancer. During cooking, the tomato **cells** break down and release the lycopene. So, a healthy **diet** contains both raw and cooked foods.

Cous cous salad makes a great meal, as it contains all the main **food groups**. Fish and beans are great sources of protein. The cous cous contains lots of **carbohydrates**, the vegetables contain **fiber** and vitamins, and the olive oil is a healthy fat.

The power of protein

Protein is a very important food group. It is found in large amounts in meat, fish, eggs, lentils, beans, and cheese. Humans and other animals are mostly made of different kinds of protein. We need to eat protein to build our bodies and to maintain them. The body's cells have to make new cells to replace old ones. Cells need proteins to build the new cells. If you cut yourself, your body uses a type of protein to mend the wound.

A little of everything

A main meal, such as lunch or dinner, should contain a good source of protein. A good meal also contains a carbohydrate food, such as pasta or potatoes, and some fresh vegetables.

This meal contains protein, carbohydrates, and vegetables. Can you spot them all?

Meat or no meat?

The human body is designed for eating meat. We have sharp cutting teeth, called **incisors** and **canine teeth**, that are good for tearing meat. In **prehistoric** times, though, people probably did not eat as much meat as we do now. They only ate it occasionally, when they could catch and kill a wild animal. Meat provides protein and many vitamins and minerals. But because it also contains unhealthy fat, it is healthier not to eat it every day.

Some people choose not to eat meat. Vegetarians eat no meat or fish, but they do eat animal products such as eggs and cheese. Vegans do not eat any meat or animal products at all.

Chopping is an essential part of preparing your own healthy food.

Knife safety

When you are cooking, you often have to chop up meat and vegetables. You need to use a really sharp cooking knife, not a normal table knife—so be careful!

- Have an adult to supervise you.

- Always chop on a chopping board.

- Always hold the knife pointing away from you, especially when carrying it.

- Keep your fingers away from the knife blade while chopping.

- Do not leave sharp knives in a sink full of water—someone might grab the blade by accident!

Steps to follow

1 Heat the oven to 350°F. Heat the olive oil in a saucepan. Add the onion and cook over a low heat for about 10 minutes until soft, stirring often. Then add the tomatoes and basil or oregano and cook for 15 minutes, stirring often. Turn off the heat and leave to cool for a few minutes.

2 Put the pita bread on to the baking sheet. Spoon the tomato sauce on to the pita bread and spread it around with the spoon. Cover each piece of pita bread almost to the edges.

3 Sprinkle grated cheese over each pizza. Then sprinkle your choice of vegetables on top.

4 Put the pizzas into the hot oven. Cook for 10 minutes until heated through.

Pita pizzas

To make two pizzas, you will need:

* 1 small chopped onion
* 1 tablespoon olive oil
* 1 cup chopped canned tomatoes
* 1 teaspoon dried basil or oregano
* 2 large whole-wheat pieces of pita bread
* 1 cup grated mozzarella cheese

Selection of prepared vegetables. Choose from:
* 1 chopped red or green pepper

* $\frac{1}{2}$ cup sliced mushrooms
* 1 tablespoon drained, pitted olives
* $\frac{1}{2}$ cup chopped broccoli
* $\frac{1}{2}$ cup chopped onion
* Sharp knife
* Chopping board
* Small saucepan
* Wooden spoon
* Baking sheet
* Oven mitts

A health-packed pizza!

People often think of pizza as an unhealthy **junk food**. Carryout or restaurant pizza can be very unhealthy. It often has too much **refined** flour, fat, **sugar**, and salt in it. However, the whole-wheat pita bread base in this pizza recipe makes it healthier. The cheese provides protein, and the pizza has lots of vitamin-packed vegetables on top.

Pita pockets

Pita bread comes from Greece—"pita" means "flat layer" in Greek. It is popular in the Mediterranean and the Middle East and is now found all over the world. A pita makes a great healthy snack. You can open it up like a pocket and fill it with cheese, beans or meat, and salad.

You can make a pita pocket sandwich like this in just a couple of minutes.

Salmon surprises

For two people, you will need:

* 2 salmon fillets
* 2 slices of lemon
* 1 teaspoon dried herbs, such as parsley or thyme
* Olive oil
* Extra-thick aluminium foil
* Baking sheet

1 Preheat the oven to 350°F.

Tear off two pieces of foil, each about 12 inches (30 cm) long. Place the foil wrappers on the baking sheet, and lay a salmon fillet in the middle of each one. Lay a lemon slice on top of each fillet and sprinkle with the herbs. Drizzle about a teaspoon of olive oil on to each fillet.

2 Pull up the sides of the foil around the salmon. Fold them over each other and crumple the foil together. Pull up the ends and crumple them in, too, until the salmon is inside a sealed package.

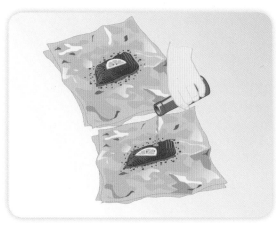

3 Put the packages into the hot oven. Ask an adult to help. Bake for about 20 minutes and serve.

- You can use foil packages to cook other types of fish, too, such as trout or haddock.
- Instead of an oven, you can cook the packages on a hot barbecue.

Fish for health

Fish contains lots of protein and is often low in fat. Some types of fish have a lot of fat, but it is a very healthy type of fat. These fish, called **oil-rich fish**, include salmon, tuna, mackerel, and sardines. Fish also contains lots of important vitamins and minerals. **Zinc** is a mineral found in fish that helps your body to **digest** other foods.

Salmon is healthy and delicious. It is good for your brain, senses, and heart, and it helps to give you healthy skin and shiny hair.

Overfishing

Some types of fish are caught so often that they become very rare. This is called **overfishing**. The fish cannot breed fast enough to build up their numbers. Overfished species include cod, sole, and orange roughy. Governments are trying to help overfished species recover by limiting the numbers of fish that fishing boats are allowed to catch.

Desserts

Steps to follow

Prepare and chop all the fruit (see table on page 23) and add to the bowl.

2 Squeeze the lemon and pour the juice into the fruit salad. Stir until all the ingredients are well mixed. You can serve the salad with yogurt.

The lemon juice stops the fruit from turning brown.

Fruit super-salad dessert

For six people, you will need:

* 1 lemon
* Selection of fruit. Choose at least eight from:
* 1 banana
* 1 pear
* 1 apple
* 2 peaches or nectarines
* Half a small melon
* 3 oranges or tangerines
* 1 cup blueberries
* 1 cup cherries
* 1 cup strawberries
* 1 cup raspberries
* 1 cup seedless grapes
* Large bowl
* Chopping board
* Sharp knife
* Wooden spoon

Fruit vitamins

Many fruits contain important **vitamins**. Vitamins are **chemicals** that help your body do various jobs. Vitamin C, for example, is found in blueberries and in citrus fruits such as oranges and grapefruits. It helps many of your **organs** to work and helps you fight off diseases.

Preparing fruit

Fruit	Preparation
Bananas	Peel and chop the banana into slices.
Pears and apples	Wash and chop into quarters from the stalk to the base. Cut out the core and seeds, then slice up the quarters.
Peaches and nectarines	Wash, cut into quarters, and pull out the pit. Slice up the quarters.
Melon	Cut into sections with a large knife. Scoop out the seeds. Cut the skin off each piece and chop the pieces up.
Blueberries	Wash and leave whole.
Cherries	Wash and remove stalks. Slice in half around the pit and scoop out the pit.
Strawberries	Wash and remove green tops. Cut in half, or slice up larger berries.
Raspberries	Wash, remove any leaves, and leave whole.
Grapes	Wash, remove any stalks, and cut in half.
Oranges or tangerines	Peel off the skin and break up into segments.

Fabulous fruit

A **fruit** is a fleshy part of a plant that grows around the plant's seeds.

Fruit is good for you. But it contains **sugar**, so you should brush your teeth after eating it. Fruit also contains lots of **fiber**, especially if you can eat the skin. Fiber helps to keep your **digestive system** working well.

Eating fruit salad for dessert is a great way to get the health benefits of many different fruits at once.

Sugary foods

Sugar is a special type of **carbohydrate** that tastes sweet. Fruits naturally contain sugar. Some other foods, such as honey and milk, naturally contain sugar, too.

Humans and many other animals are naturally programmed to like sweet foods because of the useful energy they provide.

In the body

There are many different types of sugar, but they all do the same job. They give your body energy. Energy travels around the body in the form of **glucose**, a type of sugar, in your blood. It is delivered to your **cells** to give them the energy they need to work.

Calories

You have probably heard of **calories**. A calorie is a measurement of the energy stored in a food. There are calories in all foods, but **fat** and sugar have the most calories. There are about 400 calories in half a cup of **refined** white sugar. An apple has about 50 calories, and a banana has about 100 calories.

We all need calories every day. A man needs about 2,500 calories per day, and a woman needs about 2,000. We use up calories when we move around and do things. If we take in too many calories, our body has to store the extra energy that we have not used up. It stores the energy as fat. This is why eating a lot of high-calorie food can make us gain weight.

Trouble for teeth

Sugar can also damage your teeth. The **bacteria** that cause **tooth decay** feed on sugar. After sugary foods or drinks, you should always brush your teeth. If this is not possible, chewing a small piece of cheese will help your teeth. It clears sugar from your teeth and makes saliva flow in your mouth to fight decay-causing chemicals.

When you buy packaged foods, the package will usually have a chart printed on it that tells you how many calories that food contains.

Steps to follow

Frozen yogurt

For four people, you will need:

* 3 ripe peaches or nectarines
* 2 cups natural yogurt
* 2 tablespoons honey
* Mixing bowl
* Sharp knife
* Chopping board
* Wooden spoon
* 4 small plastic cups

1 Peel the peaches or nectarines, cut into quarters, and remove the pits. Chop the quarters up finely into small pieces. Put the peaches in the mixing bowl.

2 Add all the yogurt and honey and stir well. Spoon the yogurt mixture into the cups. Put the cups in the freezer, and leave for at least two hours to freeze.

When your yogurt is frozen, you can eat it with a spoon. You can make this yogurt with other types of fruit, too, such as raspberries, pears, or bananas.

What is yogurt?

Yogurt is made from milk. It is made thick and creamy by adding a special type of bacteria, then warming it gently. The bacteria grow, and this **ferments** the milk, which changes its texture. Like all **dairy products**, such as milk, cheese, and cream, yogurt contains **protein** and **calcium**.

Yogurt can contain different amounts of fat, depending on the type of milk it was made from. Using low-fat yogurt will make a dessert extra healthy. Some yogurts also contain certain types of live bacteria that are very good for you. They help your **intestines** (part of the digestive system) to work well and **digest** food quickly. If you want this type of yogurt, look for the words "live" or "bio" on the package.

Yogurt lollipops

To make yogurt lollipops, leave the yogurt in the freezer for an hour, then stick a wooden lollipop stick (or a small teaspoon) into the middle of each one.

Yogurt uses

Even high-fat yogurt contains less fat than cream or ice cream—so it makes a great healthy dessert. Try having yogurt with fruit salad or with hot desserts such as baked apples. If you want to make it sweeter, stir in a little honey.

A worker in a yogurt factory pours fresh yogurt into a giant vat.

Drinks

Steps to follow

Warning:
Be very careful with blenders. Always have an adult to help you. Turn the blender off and unplug it as soon as you have finished using it, and never touch the blades.

Super-fit smoothies

For two people, you will need:

* 1 cup natural yogurt
* Selection of **fruit**. Choose two or three from the following:
* 2 peeled, chopped apples
* 2 peeled, chopped pears
* 2 peeled, chopped peaches or nectarines
* 1 peeled, chopped banana
* 1 cup washed, de-stalked strawberries
* 1 cup washed raspberries
* 1 cup washed blueberries
* 1 peeled, chopped mango
* Sharp knife
* Chopping board
* Blender
* 2 glasses

1 Prepare the fruit you have chosen (see page 23 for guidelines).

2 Put the fruit into the blender and add the yogurt.

3 Blend all the ingredients until smooth and pour the smoothie into two glasses.

Fruit count

You need to eat at least five helpings of fruits and **vegetables** every day to stay really healthy—and smoothies help you do that! You can fit up to three portions of fruit into one yummy smoothie. You can actually put some types of vegetables in, too, if you like. Peeled, sliced cucumber makes a smoothie extra refreshing.

Soft ingredients only!

Remember, a blender can only blend soft fruits and vegetables with no hard skins, pits, or stalks. Do not use very hard foods such as raw carrots.

Dairy-free smoothies

The smoothies in this recipe contain yogurt. It adds to the taste, makes the smoothie thicker and creamier, and contains healthy **protein** and **calcium**. However, you can make smoothies without the yogurt. To keep them thick and smooth, make sure you include a banana.

A smoothie makes a refreshing drink in the summer. You can also have a smoothie with your breakfast or serve smoothies at a party.

Homemade lemonade

For a pitcher of lemonade, you will need:

* 4 unwaxed lemons
* 1 cup unrefined raw cane brown sugar
* 2 cups boiling water
* 1¼ cups cold water
* Ice cubes
* Lemon zester or grater
* Large heatproof pan
* Heatproof measuring cup
* Sharp knife
* Chopping board
* Wooden spoon
* Lemon juicer
* Glasses
* Serving pitcher

1 Wash and dry the lemons. Scrape the zest (the yellow part of the skin) from the lemons using the lemon zester or the fine side of a grater. Put the zest in the heatproof pan.

2 Add the sugar to the zest in the pan. Boil 2 cups of water. Pour the water into the pan with the lemon zest and sugar. Stir well with a wooden spoon until the sugar has dissolved.

3 Cut and then squeeze the lemons and add the juice to the pan. Then add 1¼ cups of cold water and stir well.

4 Put the lemonade in a pitcher in the refrigerator to chill for at least an hour. Serve it in glasses, with a few ice cubes in each one.

Lemon and lime

Try making your own lemon and lime drink by replacing two of the lemons in this recipe with four limes. (You will need more limes because they are smaller than lemons.)

Homemade is healthier

When you make your own lemonade drink, you can be sure it only contains fresh lemons and natural ingredients. Unfortunately, many drinks that you can buy in stores contain **additives** such as artificial **preservatives** and colors. Scientists think many of these chemicals can be bad for us.

Across the world, people drink billions of carbonated soda drinks every day. Besides being unhealthy, these drinks usually come in bottles or cans that add to the world's litter problems.

Sugar facts

Although this lemonade recipe is better for you than a store-bought carbonated colored drink, it does still contain sugar. Too much sugar is bad for your teeth and can contain too much energy. This is stored as **fat**—so don't drink lemonade all the time.

Steps to follow

1 Pour the tropical fruit juice into the large bowl.

2 ⚠️ Put the strawberries in the small bowl. Use the fork to mash them until they form a soft mush. Add them to the juice in the large bowl and stir well.

3 ⚠️ Prepare the rest of the fruit and add it to the large bowl. The punch can now be stored in the refrigerator until you are ready to use it. You can put a plate or plastic wrap on top of it to keep it covered.

4 Just before serving the punch, pour in the bottle of sparkling water. Add some fresh, washed mint leaves and some ice cubes. You can serve the punch by using a large ladle to pour it into glasses.

Party punch

For a large bowl of punch, you will need:

* 1 liter (2 pint) carton of tropical fruit juice
* 2 cups washed strawberries
* 1 liter (2 pint) bottle of sparkling water
* Mint leaves
* Ice cubes

A selection of other fruits. Choose from:
* 1 cup washed raspberries
* 1 peeled, sliced peach
* 1 sliced apple
* 1 sliced orange
* Large glass bowl
* Small bowl
* Fork
* Sharp knife
* Chopping board
* Wooden spoon
* Ladle

Party time!

This punch recipe is great for parties. As you serve it, try to add a few pieces of fruit, a mint leaf, and an ice cube for each person. The fruit makes the punch healthier and prettier. Although the punch does contain carbonated water, it is diluted by the juice, so it is still quite healthy.

Design your own punch

This punch uses tropical fruit juice, but you could experiment with using other types—such as orange juice, mango juice, or apple juice.

Each glass of punch contains a selection of healthy fruit as well as a refreshing drink.

Snacks

Trail mix

To make about 15 2-ounce (55-g) servings, you will need:

* 1 cup breakfast **cereal** shapes, such as **whole-grain** hoops
* $\frac{1}{2}$ cup raisins
* $\frac{1}{2}$ cup dried apricots
* 1 cup sunflower seeds
* 1 cup chocolate chips
* $\frac{2}{3}$ cup unsalted cashew nuts, hazelnuts, or almonds
* $\frac{2}{3}$ cup dried banana slices
* Sharp knife
* Chopping board
* Large bowl
* Wooden spoon
* Zip-top bags

1 Chop up the dried apricots into smaller pieces.

2 Mix all the ingredients together in the large bowl.

3 Weigh out ¼ cup portions into zip-top bags. Store the trail mix in the refrigerator until you want to use it.

Nut allergies

Some people have serious **allergies** to nuts. If they eat them, or sometimes even if they go near them, they can get very sick. If you know anyone with a nut allergy, do not take your trail mix to any activity they will be attending. Alternatively, you can make your trail mix without the nuts.

What is trail mix?

Trail mix gets its name because it was invented as a snack for people who are on the move—for example, climbing, trekking, or hiking along a trail. The nuts, seeds, dried **fruit**, and chocolate in trail mix contain a lot of energy. Nuts and seeds also contain healthy **fats** and **protein**. The fruit contains **fiber**, **vitamins**, and **minerals**.

High-energy snacks

Each 2-ounce (55-g) bag of trail mix contains about 250 **calories**. That is a lot of calories for a snack. (An apple contains around 50 calories and a slice of bread 80 to 100 calories.) However, you need high-energy snacks when you use up a lot of energy—for example, when you play sports.

Hiking is great exercise, especially if it includes climbing up a steep hill.

Energy, calories, and exercise

The energy in food is measured in calories. When you eat food, you take in calories (see page 25). For example, if you eat a big plate of pasta with tomato sauce and cheese on top, you will take in about 550 calories.

When you do things—like walking, running, thinking, or even sitting doing nothing—you use calories up. If you cycle for an hour, you will use about 550 calories. If you just sit on a sofa and watch TV for an hour, you'll use around 90 calories.

Getting calories right

The more exercise you get, the more calories you need. Snacks between meals can help you take in more calories when you need them. If you have too many high-calorie snacks and do not exercise enough, you will gain weight. The extra energy you do not use will be stored as fat on your body.

Walking or cycling to places instead of using a car, taking stairs instead of elevators, and dancing at parties are all ways you can get more exercise.

What's wrong with fat?

We all need some fat on our bodies. It cushions our bones and **organs** and acts as a store of energy. In fact, an average healthy person's body is about 18 to 25 percent fat. But if too much fat builds up on our bodies, it can be unhealthy. It can cause illnesses such as heart disease.

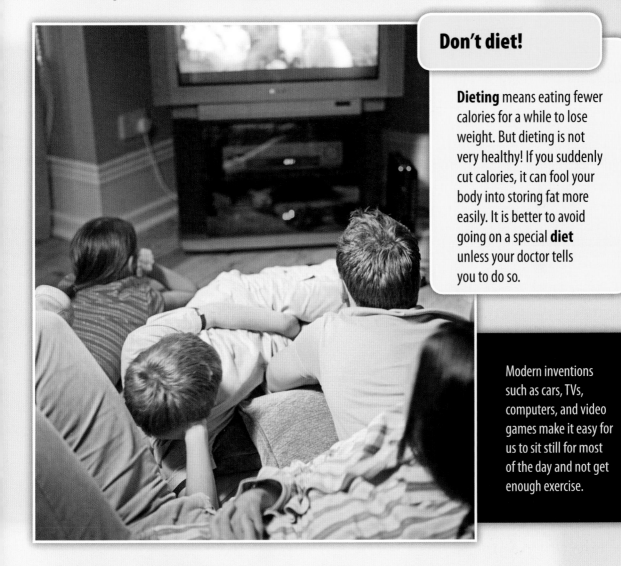

Don't diet!

Dieting means eating fewer calories for a while to lose weight. But dieting is not very healthy! If you suddenly cut calories, it can fool your body into storing fat more easily. It is better to avoid going on a special **diet** unless your doctor tells you to do so.

Modern inventions such as cars, TVs, computers, and video games make it easy for us to sit still for most of the day and not get enough exercise.

Exercise every day

The best way to stay healthy is to eat mainly healthy food and get lots of exercise. This means that any spare calories you eat will get used up. Exercise is also good for you. It keeps your body in shape, builds up your muscles, and makes you feel good.

Snack science

There are many different snacks to choose from. There are plenty of options for healthy snacks, too.

Snack sorter

Which of these snacks do you think are the healthiest, and which are less healthy? Which contain the most calories? Do you know which **food groups** are in each snack?

Iced doughnut

Hummus dip with vegetable sticks

Carrot

Bowl of potato chips

Apple

Trail mix

Chocolate bar

Which is which?

Iced doughnut: 300 calories

This is an unhealthy snack with too many calories. It contains a lot of **sugar** and is usually fried in an unhealthy type of fat.

Carrot: About 20 calories

A carrot contains healthy fiber, vitamins, and water, but it has so few calories that it will not keep you going for long. It is a good snack if you are not getting much exercise but feel like eating—for example, while watching TV.

Apple: 50 calories

An apple contains fiber, vitamins, water, and some sugar. It makes a good quick snack without overloading on calories.

Chocolate bar: 250 calories in a 2-ounce (55-g) bar

Chocolate is mainly fat and sugar. It has a lot of calories, so it is not very healthy. However, it is better for your teeth than sticky sweet snacks such as raisins because it melts away quickly. It is OK in very small amounts.

Hummus dip with vegetable sticks: 220 calories

This snack has lots of calories, but contains chickpeas and sesame seeds, which are full of protein and healthy **carbohydrates**.

Bowl of potato chips: About 140 calories in a 1-ounce (28-g) bag

Potato chips contain a lot of calories, fat, salt, and sometimes sugar, too. They are quite unhealthy and it is best to avoid them.

Trail mix: 250 calories in a 2-ounce (55-g) bag

Like hummus, this is a healthy snack when you need a high-calorie boost. It contains nuts, seeds, and fruits that are full of protein, natural sugar, and good fat.

Healthy and Happy

Healthy eating is not about missing out. It is just about making sure you get lots of great ingredients into your food, to make it as good for you as it can be. As this book shows, you can make all kinds of food healthier—from pizzas and kebabs to desserts, drinks, and snacks. So, you can eat lots of the foods you like but be healthy, too.

Healthy food should not be boring or taste bad. It should be delicious and make you feel great.

Help your body

We all want our bodies to look good, work well, and give us a long and happy life. By eating healthily, you can help that happen. Healthy food will make your body work better, so that you feel great, can do more, and do not feel sick as often. Scientists have even found that healthy eating helps you do better at schoolwork and on exams. On top of all that, healthy foods can help to give you clear, glowing skin, healthy teeth, and shiny hair.

Be involved with your food

It is great to get into the habit of preparing and cooking your own food. It is healthier because you use fresh ingredients. You will also leave out the **preservatives**, food colorings, artificial sweeteners, and other **additives** found in many ready-made foods. You can also use the ingredients you like best, so you are in control.

How much unhealthy food is unhealthy?

Everyone sometimes wants an unhealthy snack—like a chocolate, a handful of chips, or a slice of cake at a party. Experts have found that if you ban a food completely, you will probably want it more. As long as you eat healthy food most of the time, unhealthy foods are OK once in a while.

Party!

In addition to everyday eating, the healthy foods in this book are great for parties, picnics, and barbecues. Try making a feast for your friends or family next time you have a birthday party, vacation, or family gathering.

When you eat healthily, your body will pay you back by helping you be the best you can be at sports, games, and tests.

Glossary

acidic containing an acid, which is a type of chemical. Acidic substances are bad for your teeth.

additive chemical added to food. Additives include preservatives and food colorings.

allergy illness, rash, or other symptom often caused by eating or being near a certain type of food. For example, some people have an allergic reaction to nuts.

bacteria microscopic living things found in many places, including in our bodies and in some foods. Some types of bacteria are harmful to us, but others can be helpful.

bran tough outer layers of a grain. Bran contains a lot of fiber.

calcium mineral that helps to build healthy teeth and bones. Milk contains calcium.

calorie unit of energy. Calories are used to measure the amount of energy found in food.

canine teeth sharp, pointed teeth. Canine teeth are good for tearing meat.

carbohydrate type of food chemical or food group. Carbohydrates contain a lot of energy and provide fuel for the body.

cell one of the building blocks that all living things are made from. Your cells need energy to make them work.

cereal another name for a food made from grains. Rice and wheat are cereals.

chemical substance made up of atoms and molecules. Food, like other materials, is made from chemicals.

dairy product food made from milk. Cheese, cream, and butter are all dairy products.

diet foods you eat, or the foods you are in the habit of eating. A healthy diet includes fresh vegetables.

dieting choosing to eat less food or food with fewer calories in it. People often diet to try to lose weight.

digest break down food into useful chemicals that can be used by the body. Your digestive system digests your food.

digestive system set of organs in the body that take in and digest food. Your digestive system includes your mouth, stomach, and intestines.

fat type of food chemical or food group. Butter, oil, and fried foods all contain fats.

ferment go through a chemical change caused by living cells, such as bacteria or yeast. Yogurt is a fermented food.

fiber substance found in some foods. Fiber is made from the tough parts of plants that cannot be digested.

food group type of food, based on the types of chemicals it contains and what they do for the body. The main food groups include carbohydrates and proteins.

fruit soft, fleshy part of a plant usually found around the seed or seeds. Fruits are part of a healthy diet.

germ tiny living thing, such as bacteria, that can invade the body and cause diseases. Raw meat can contain harmful germs.

glucose type of sugar. The body uses glucose to transport energy to all its cells.

grain type of food made from the seeds of grass-like plants. Oats, wheat, rice, and barley are grains.

husk rough covering that surrounds some types of grain. Husks are high in fiber.

hydrogenated fat fat that has been chemically changed to make it easier to cook with. Hydrogenated fats are unhealthy.

incisor sharp, flat-edged cutting tooth. The incisors are found at the front of the mouth.

intestines long tubes in the digestive system. The intestines soak up food chemicals and carry away waste.

iron type of mineral found in meat and some other foods. Iron helps the blood to carry oxygen.

junk food cheap, popular, high-calorie food. Junk food is not very healthy.

lycopene chemical found in some red foods. Lycopene helps the body fight off illness.

mineral useful chemical found in food. Iron and salt are both minerals.

oil-rich fish fish that contains healthy fat. Salmon and mackerel are oil-rich fish.

organ body part that does a particular job. The heart and brain are organs.

overfishing fishing for one type of fish so much that its numbers fall sharply. Overfishing has affected cod stocks.

prehistoric from the time before historical records were written down. Prehistoric people often gathered wild nuts and fruit.

preservative chemical added to foods to make them last longer. Some preservatives can be bad for you.

protein type of food chemical or food group. Proteins help to build body parts and repair our bodies.

refined processed to remove unwanted parts such as grain husks. White sugar has been refined.

sugar type of carbohydrate that tastes sweet. Sugar contains a lot of energy.

sweat liquid released by the skin to help the body to cool down. Sweat contains mostly water.

tooth decay damage caused to the teeth by bacteria. The bacteria make acid that eats away at the tooth surface, making it rot away.

trans-fat fat that has been chemically altered to make it longer-lasting and easier to cook with. Trans-fats are not healthy.

urine liquid waste from the body. Urine carries waste chemicals out of the blood.

vegetable food made from part of a plant such as the stalk, root, or leaves. Celery and cabbage are vegetables.

vitamin type of useful chemical found in food. For example, vitamin C is found in oranges.

whole-grain food made with unrefined grains. Whole-grains have not had any of their parts, such as the husk and bran, removed.

zinc mineral found in some foods. Zinc is good for the digestive system.

Find Out More

Books

Ballard, Carol. *Healthy Body—Eating Right.* Farmington Hills, Mich.: Blackbirch, 2004.

This book explains how healthy eating works and which foods are the healthiest.

Buller, Laura. *Food (Eyewitness* series). New York: Dorling Kindersley, 2005.

Detailed information about every aspect of food, with lots of photos and pictures.

Claybourne, Anna. *The Usborne Complete Book of the Human Body.* Tulsa, Okla.: Usborne/EDC, 2006.

The science of how your body works, including why it needs food.

Miller, Edward. *The Monster Health Book: A Guide to Eating Healthy, Being Active, & Feeling Great for Monsters & Kids!* New York: Holiday House, 2006.

A fun guide to healthy eating and exercise.

Simon, Seymour. *Guts: Our Digestive System.* New York: HarperCollins, 2005.

How the intestines —also called the guts—work to take food into your body.

Sohn, Emily. *Food and Nutrition.* New York: Chelsea House, 2006.

Learn more about how your food choices affect your health.

Spilsbury, Louise. *Why Should I Eat This Carrot?: And Other Questions About Healthy Eating.* Chicago: Heinemann Library, 2004.

This book answers lots of interesting questions about healthy foods.

Websites

U.S. Department of Agriculture—For Kids

www.mypyramid.gov/kids/

Test your knowledge of healthy eating with a variety of games and worksheets.

Health and exercise quiz

www.kidzworld.com/quiz/2851-quiz-eating-and-exercise-trivia

Test your health knowledge.

Kidnetic

www.kidnetic.com

Food and fitness site for kids, with recipes, quizzes, and activities.

KidsHealth

http://kidshealth.org/kid/stay_healthy/food/pyramid.html

Lots of facts about all aspects of health, exercise, and healthy eating.

The Food Museum Online

www.foodmuseum.com

Food facts, news, and history, with multimedia exhibits.

Index